UNBREAK-ABLE
AND BECOMING

A friendly, modern, and practical guide for women embracing self-worth, freedom, and emotional freedom with kindness.

ZANDRA MAE COCHRANE

UBREAKABLE AND BECOMING

WRITTEN BY ZANDRA MAE COCHRANE
ISBN: 978-1-764463O-O-3

ALL RIGHTS RESERVED. NO PART OF THIS BOOK MAY BE REPRODUCED, STORED IN A RETRIEVAL SYSTEM, OR TRANSMITTED IN ANY FORM OR BY ANY MEANS— ELECTRONIC, MECHANICAL, PHOTOCOPYING, RECORDING, OR OTHERWISE—WITHOUT PRIOR WRITTEN PERMISSION OF THE PUBLISHER.

FIRST EDITION, 2O25

love, peace, and joy

FROM THIS YEAR 2026

You are worth it!

INTRODUCTION
Why this book matter?

Have you ever found yourself questioning your own worth? Many women — regardless of age, background, or relationship status — have quietly asked, "Am I really enough?" or "Do I deserve better?" These questions often arise not because we are weak, but because we have spent years giving too much, loving too hard, or carrying emotional weight that was never ours to hold.

In today's world, countless women feel drained by relationships, overwhelmed by self-doubt, or pressured to perform and "hold everything together." Even long before now, women have struggled with internal insecurities, silent emotional battles, and the fear of speaking their truth. You may have people around you — friends, family, or a partner — yet still feel alone with your thoughts. And for many, opening up about self-worth feels difficult, uncomfortable, or even unsafe.

This book was created as your gentle companion on the journey back to yourself. It is not a heavy textbook or a strict program. Instead, it's a friendly, one to two-page-per-chapter guide filled with practical strategies, mindset shifts, reflection prompts, and fun challenges that support real emotional healing. Think of it as a blend of a mentor's handbook and a trusted friend's reassurance — the kind that reminds you of your strength even on the days you forget it.

Throughout these pages, you'll learn how to rebuild your self-worth from the inside out, set healthy boundaries without guilt, and embrace emotional freedom in a way that feels natural and stress-free. Every chapter is simple, actionable, and crafted to help you reconnect with the version of yourself who is confident, deserving, and deeply worthy of love — especially your own.

CHAPTER I
Understanding Self-Worth Without Overthinking

According to key concepts, Self-worth is defined as a deep belief that you are valuable simply because you exist. It's not tied to achievements, appearance, or other people's approval. Many of us are confused between this two important terms: Self Worth and Self-esteem.

- Self-esteem refers on how you feel about your skills, talents, or accomplishments.
- Self-worth means knowing you deserve love, respect, and peace regardless of what you achieve.

Why it is significant? because without self-worth, you may overthink, doubt yourself, or settle for less than you deserve. When you don't believe in your own value, you may find yourself being trapped in cycles of pleasing people around, tolerating unhealthy behaviors, or keeping in silence your own needs. This often leads to exhaustion, anxiety, and a sense of being invisible.

However, with self-worth, you begin to see yourself as someone worthy of respect, love, and joy. You stop measuring your value by achievements or other people's approval, and instead anchor it in your own truth. **Self-worth gives you the opportunity and strength to say "no" when something drains you, and "yes" when something aligns with your growth.** It helps you build resilience in the face of setbacks, confidence in your decisions, and healthier relationships where mutual respect is the foundation.

Think of self-worth as the soil in which everything else grows: your boundaries, your confidence, your peace, and your ability to thrive. When the soil is rich, your life blossoms. When it's neglected, everything struggles to take root. That's why nurturing self-worth is not optional — it's essential for living a life that feels whole, balanced, and authentically yours. With **self-worth**, you build resilience, confidence, and healthier relationships.

Now these are some of the signs of Low Self-Worth that I have personally encountered and experienced:
- Constantly apologizng, even when you've done nothing wrong.
- Difficulty of saying "no" and setting boundaries.
- Seeking validation from others before making decisions.

- Ignoring your own needs to please others.
- Feeling "not enough" no matter how much you achieve and made efforts.

Here are some of the Practical Tips:
- Pause when you catch yourself in self-criticism. Replace the thought with kindness.
- Practice saying: "I am enough" daily in front of a mirror.
- Surround yourself with people who uplift you, not those who drain your energy.
- Keep a "Worth Journal" or Diary if you can — write one thing each day that proves your value beyond achievements.

Gentle exercises for yourself

I have written below some gentle questions for yourself. You can grab any piece of paper for you to write it down or think for a moment.

- When do I feel most valuable?
- Write down 5 qualities about yourself that have nothing to do with achievements (e.g., kindness, creativity, resilience, humor, empathy).
- Create a "Self-Worth Circle" — draw a circle and fill it with words or doodles that represent your strengths and values.

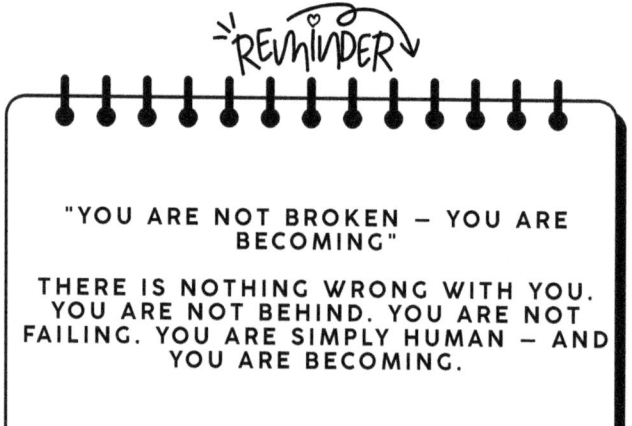

"I am worthy, simply because I am me".

AFFIRMATION

CHAPTER 2
Recognizing Draining or Toxic Relationships

Relationships are meant to be sources of support, joy, and growth. At one point, it give us energy, encouragement, motivation and a sense of belonging. They help us feel seen, valued, and safe. Yet sometimes, not all of us, we find ourselves in connections that leave us feeling drained rather than nourished. These are the relationships where you just wanted to walk away because you felt smaller, heavier, or less confident than before. Recognizing these draining or toxic relationships is a vital step in protecting your self-worth.

Toxic relationships don't always announce themselves loudly. Often, they show up in subtle patterns that slowly takes away your confidence over time. We often termed and hear this as **"Red Flags"**. These are some common signs of it:

- Constant criticism in which you feel judged more than supported.
- Lack of respect where your opinions, time, or boundaries are dismissed.
- Manipulation in which you're being guilt-tripped or pressured into choices that don't feel right.
- Ignoring boundaries where your requests for space, boundary or limits are being disregarded.
- Neglecting your feelings where you're being told as "too sensitive" or just "overreacting."
- Guilt for having needs, that is when you feel selfish simply for asking for care or respect.

Why all of this matter? Simply because when you stay in draining relationships, you begin to doubt yourself, compromise your values, and lose energy for the things that truly matter. It slowly or may loose all your confidence. You will end up overthinking and questioning some things in yourself that doesn't have to or need to. Worst is, you will just keep silence for the word you believed **"Peace"** in which you never had it.

Healthy relationships, on the other hand, uplift you, encourage your growth, and respect your boundaries. They encourage your growth, respect your boundaries, and celebrate your individuality. They leave you feeling lighter, stronger, and more aligned with your true self. Choosing to recognize and step back from toxic dynamics is not selfish — it's an act of self-respect. It's saying: **"My peace matters. My worth matters."**

Think of relationships as mirrors. The healthy ones reflect back your strengths, your joy, and your potential. The unhealthy ones distract your reflection, making you believe you are less than you truly are. As your guide, I encourage you to trust your inner signals or we sometimes call it "instincts". If you consistently feel drained, anxious, or unworthy after being with someone, that's valuable information. Your feelings are not overreactions — they are wisdom pointing you toward change. This is not just to boyfriend or girlfriend or husband and wife, it could maybe surrounding you as friends, workmates, careers and so forth.

Gentle exercises for yourself

The Peace Check

Let us check your peace. You can grab any piece of paper or note if you want to write down or pause a moment if you wanted to while finding answers to some questions. Again, your emotions are powerful signals. Let us say, after spending time with someone, pause and ask yourself:
- Do I feel lighter or heavier?
- Do I feel respected or dismissed?
- Do I feel energized or emotionally exhausted?

If the answer consistently leans toward "heavier" or "exhausted," this is a sign the relationship may be draining your peace. I wanted you to take a note on this and have a bit more time to reflect on this. I know you can do it.

Reflections

Create two lists:

1. People who lift you — those who make you feel valued, joyful, and safe.
2. People who drain you — those who leave you anxious, guilty, or unworthy.

Seeing these lists side by side helps you visualize where your energy is flowing and where it's being taken away.

Relationship Energy Audit

1. Circle or write one draining relationship from your list.
2. Brainstorm one small boundary you can set today. Examples:
    - Limit the time you spend with them.
    - Say: "I'm not available right now."
    - Choose not to engage in conversations that make you feel small or anhthing you felt it may help your inner space.
3. Write down how you expect to feel after setting this boundary (lighter, calmer, more in control).

CHAPTER 3
Gentle Healing: Releasing the past with kindness

Are you familiar with the saying, "Time heals all wounds"? I've heard it from a beautiful singer with the lyrics, "Time heals all wounds, they say, and I should know, but it seems like forever, now I'm letting you go". Now, healing isn't about pretending the pain never happened. It's about learning to carry it differently, until it no longer weighs or let you down. Many women carry wounds from toxic relationships, childhood experiences, or moments where they felt unseen. These pain can show up in everyday life — overthinking a text message, feeling guilty for saying "no," or replaying old arguments in your head.

Gentle healing means giving yourself permission to move forward without rushing or forcing. It's about small, steady steps that help you reclaim that peace.

These are some steps to process emotional pain or being emotionally hurt gently:

- First, acknowledge the pain. For example, you might say, "Yes, that breakup or person hurt me deeply. I don't need to reduce that pain." Naming the pain validates your experience.
- Name your feelings. Instead of saying "I'm fine,"or "I'm okay" write down: "I feel angry that my boundaries and feelings were ignored. I feel sad that I wasn't valued."
- Give yourself permission to rest. Healing can be exhausting. If you notice you're drained after talking about the past, allow yourself to pause and do something soothing — like a walk, a bath, watch movies, go to church or journaling.
- Seek safe outlets. Many women find relief in journaling, painting, or talking to a trusted friend. For example, instead of bottling up anger, you might write a letter you'll never send.
- Take small steps: Healing doesn't happen overnight. Celebrate progress like being able to say "no" once, or going a whole day without replaying the past.

Forgiveness vs. Forgetting

Imagine you're carrying a heavy backpack filled with stones. Each stone represents a hurtful memory — a betrayal, a harsh word, a broken promise. Forgiveness is choosing to put the backpack down. The stones don't disappear; they still exist. But you stop carrying them everywhere you go.

In real life, forgiveness might look like this:
- You decide to stop replaying an argument with a friend who let you down.
- You acknowledge the pain of a breakup, but you choose not to let it define your future relationships.
- You release resentment toward a parent, family member, trusted friend who couldn't give you the love you needed, while still recognizing the impact it had.

Forgiveness is not about saying, "What happened was okay." It's about saying, "I deserve peace more than I deserve to carry this anger." It's a gift you give yourself — freedom from the weight of the past.

Gentle exercises for yourself

Mini Exercises for Releasing Trauma

a. **Letter of Release:** Write a letter to the person or situation that hurt you. For example: "You made me feel small, but I now choose to let go of that pain." Tear it up or burn it safely as a symbol of release.

b. **Body Scan Meditation:** Notice where you hold tension — maybe in your shoulders after remembering an argument. Breathe deeply and imagine exhaling that weight.

c. **Symbolic Ritual:** Write one painful memory on paper. For example: "The day I felt abandoned." Tear it up and throw it away. This act helps your mind release the grip of that memory.

d. **Affirmation Practice:** Stand in front of a mirror and say: "I release what no longer serves me. I deserve peace." Repeat until you feel calmer.

"

I release the past with kindness, and I welcome peace into my present."

AFFIRMATION

CHAPTER 4
Single, Whole & Worthy

Being Single Is Powerful, not a Failure. I know some of you here may not agree with me but many women or men are taught to see singlehood as a gap — something to be ashamed of or "fixed." To others, it is a requirement in order to feel free. But being single is not a failure or a requirement ;nor is it a sign that something is wrong with you. Actually it's an opportunity. It's simply one of life's seasons — a form of time off or space you choose for yourself. Just as we take breaks from work to recharge, singlehood can be a break from the demands of relationships, giving you room to breathe, reflect, and grow. It's a personal choice rooted from personal perspectives in life. It's a season where you can focus on yourself without compromise, rediscover your passions, and build a life that feels authentic.

This season doesn't mean you're incomplete. It means you're giving yourself the gift of clarity and freedom. You're learning to enjoy your own company, to listen to your inner voice, and to build a life that feels authentic.

Think of it as a pause button, not a stop sign. It's not about waiting for someone else to arrive; it's about using the space to reconnect with yourself. When you step into future relationships, you'll do so from a place of strength, not need. honestly, relationships can add joy, but they will or don't define your worth.

Being single is not about isolation — it's about intention. It's choosing space when you need it, choosing freedom when you crave it, and choosing yourself when you deserve it. This season is powerful because it teaches you that your worth isn't tied to anyone else. **You are already whole, already worthy, and already enough.**

Fun Solo Activities

Singlehood is a chance to explore joy on your own terms:
- Take yourself out for brunch or a movie — enjoy the freedom of choosing exactly what you want.
- Try creative hobbies like painting, journaling, or photography.
- Create self-care rituals: spa nights, yoga, or meditation.
- Plan solo adventures: a day trip, a hike, or exploring a new café.
- Learn something new: a short course, a skill, or an empowering book.

Reflection

Write down three activities you've always wanted to try but postponed because you were waiting for someone else to join you.

A 7-Day "Date Yourself" Challenge

This challenge helps you practice treating yourself with the same love and attention you'd give to a partner.

- Day 1: Write yourself a love letter — list your strengths, weaknesses and what you admire about yourself.
- Day 2: Take yourself out for coffee or tea. Sit, savor, and enjoy your own company.
- Day 3: Create a playlist of songs that make you feel empowered. Dance or sing along.
- Day 4: Cook a meal just for you — set the table beautifully, light a candle, and enjoy.
- Day 5: Do something creative — paint, journal, or design a vision board.
- Day 6: Plan a solo adventure — visit a park, beach, or new part of town.
- Day 7: End with reflection. Write down what you learned about yourself this week and how it felt to prioritize your own joy.

There is no harm in trying and you don't need to explain all these stuffs to anyone. The genuine people will truly understand you. I've been there. Trust me.

"

I am single, whole, and worthy. My joy begins with me, and my space is my strength.

AFFIRMATION

CHAPTER 5
Simple Daily Habits to Rebuild Self-Worth

Many people believed that rebuilding self-worth requires dramatic or abrupt changes, but the truth is that it's the small, consistent intentional habits that make the biggest difference. Just like watering a plant daily that can helps thrive, and nurturing yourself with simple with intent habits it builds resilience and confidence over time.

Imagine waking up and immediately checking your phone. You start the day reacting to others. Now imagine this habit instead, take two minutes to breathe, stretch, and say, "I am enough." That tiny shift could sets a completely different tone for your day. The goal is not perfection, but consistency.

Morning rituals anchors your day. The way you begin your morning often shapes how the rest of your day unfolds. A simple ritual — like journaling one intention, sipping tea or coffee mindfully, or writing down three things you're grateful for — reminds you that your needs matter. Morning rituals don't have to be long or complicated. Even one minute of intentional breathing can anchor you in self-respect.

Affirmations can transform your inner voice. Your inner voice shapes how you see yourself. If it's filled with criticism, your confidence shrinks. Affirmations are short, powerful statements that replace self-doubt with self-belief. Instead of thinking, "I'm not good enough," you practice saying, "I am worthy of love and respect." Over time, your brain begins to accept this truth.

Mirror Pep-Talks build confidence and gratitude. Looking into your own eyes and speaking kindly to yourself may feel awkward at first, but it's a powerful way to reconnect with your worth. It's like becoming your own best friend. Before a stressful meeting or work, you stand in front of the mirror and say, "You've got this. You are capable." That pep-talk shifts your mindset from fear to confidence.

Gratitude can shifts focus From lack to Strength. When you practice gratitude, you train your mind to notice what's working instead of what's missing. This builds resilience and helps you see yourself as resourceful and strong. Instead of ending the day thinking, "I didn't finish everything," you pause and write, "I showed up, I tried, and I learned, "I handled a tough situation with patience. I showed up even when I am tired. I asked for help when I needed it." This reframes the day with self-compassion.

- Reflection creates awareness without pressure. Reflection is about noticing patterns, not judging yourself. Asking gentle questions like, "What did I do today that honored me? ", "Where did I show strength or kindness?".

Reflection is not about finding flaws — it's about celebrating growth. Even small acts of self-respect count.

How to Track Progress Without Pressure

Progress isn't measured by how perfectly you complete habits, but by how consistently you return to them. Tracking progress should feel supportive, not stressful.

- Simple Habit Tracker: Use a notebook or printable with checkboxes for daily habits (affirmation, gratitude, reflection).
- Weekly Reflection: Instead of measuring success by numbers, ask: "Do I feel lighter, more confident, or more peaceful than last week?"
- Celebrate Small Wins: Even one day of practicing a habit is progress.

Progress is not about perfection. It's about noticing growth. Some days you'll do all the habits, some days only one — both count.

Gentle exercises for yourself

- Create a "Daily Worth Ritual" — choose 3 micro habits (e.g., affirmation, gratitude, mirror pep-talk). Practice them each day for one week.
- At the end of the week, journal: "What changed in how I see myself?"

Self-worth is rebuilt in the quiet moments: the breath you take before reacting, the kind word you speak to yourself, the gratitude you write or remember before bed. These habits may seem small, but together they create a foundation of strength, reminding you daily that you are worthy, whole, and enough.

"Small steps build my strength daily. I am worthy of love, peace, and growth."

AFFIRMATION

A day in *my life*

CHAPTER 6
Setting boundaries with Love and Clarity

Boundaries plays a significant role in terms of achieving Emotional Safety. These are not walls to shut people out — they are doors that help you decide what comes in and what stays out. It protect your emotional safety by ensuring your needs, values, and limits are respected. Without boundaries, you may feel drained, resentful, or invisible but with boundaries, you create relationships built on mutual respect.

Think of boundaries as teaching others how to treat you. For example, if a friend constantly calls late at night and you feel exhausted, setting a boundary like "I don't take calls after 9 PM" protects your rest and communicates your needs clearly.

Moreover, boundaries build Self-Worth. Every time you set a boundary, you affirm: "My needs matter. My peace matters." Boundaries are acts of self-respect. They remind you that you are worthy of love and care without sacrificing yourself. By simply saying "No thank you" when pressured into an event you don't want to attend shows that you value your time and energy.

Healthy boundaries don't push people away — they create clarity. When others know your limits, they can interact with you in ways that feel safe and respectful. This reduces misunderstandings and builds trust. For example, telling your partner, "I need space to recharge after work," helps them understand your rhythm instead of misinterpreting your silence.

Setting boundaries can be felt intimidating, especially if you've spent years putting others first or avoiding conflict. The good news is that boundaries don't have to be complicated. Short, clear statements are often the most powerful. Think of these scripts as training wheels — simple phrases that help you practice saying "no" or expressing your needs without guilt. I'll share to you some of the starter scripts you can try practicing.

a. Practice saying "No thank you." It's polite, brief, and firm. You don't owe anyone a long explanation. For example, a coworker asks you to stay late again, but you're exhausted. Instead of over-explaining, you simply say, "No thank you." This communicates respect for yourself while keeping the tone kind.

b. "I need space right now." It communicates your need without blaming the other person. For example, a friend wants to talk immediately after a stressful day, but you're not ready. You say, "I need space right now." This sets a boundary while showing that the relationship still matters.

c. "I'm not available for that." It's clear, respectful, and leaves no room for negotiation.
For example, someone invites you to an event that doesn't align with your values or energy. Instead of making excuses, you say, "I'm not available for that." This honors your time and priorities.

d. "That doesn't work for me". It affirms your choice without apology. You're stating a fact, not asking permission. For example, a family member pressures you to handle something you're uncomfortable with. You respond, "That doesn't work for me." This shows self-respect and clarity without hostility.

Boundaries don't require long explanations. In fact, over-explaining often weakens your message and invites debate. Short, clear statements are powerful because they communicate confidence. Remember: saying "no" is not rude — it's self-care.

Practice these scripts in front of a mirror or write them in your journal. The more familiar they feel, the easier it will be to use them in real situations.

Gentle exercises for yourself

Boundary-Building Worksheet

Use this worksheet to practice identifying and setting boundaries:
1. Identify the Situation
    - Where do you feel drained, disrespected, or overwhelmed?
    - Example: "My coworker keeps asking me to cover their tasks."
2. Name the Need
    - What do you need to feel safe or respected?
    - Example: "I need to protect my workload and time."
3. Choose a Script
    - Select a simple phrase to communicate your boundary.
    - Example: "I can't take on extra tasks right now."
4. Reflect
    - How did it feel to set this boundary?
    - Did it bring relief, clarity, or peace?

Boundaries are not selfish — they are essential. They teach others how to love you well and remind you that your peace is worth protecting. Start small, practice often, and remember: every boundary you set is a step toward stronger self-worth.

"My boundaries protect my peace. I set them with love and clarity."
AFFIRMATION

CHAPTER 7
Reconnecting With Your Inner Voice

Listen to your intuition and emotions. Your inner voice is the quiet guide that often knows the truth before your mind catches up. It speaks through intuition — a gut feeling you felt when something feels right or wrong — and through emotions, it may act as signals.

Intuition is not magic; it's your inner wisdom built from experience and values. For example, if you feel uneasy around someone who constantly dismisses you, that discomfort is your inner voice saying, "This isn't safe for me."

Like for example, you're offered a new opportunity. Your mind lists pros and cons, but your body feels tense. That tension is a sign to pause and listen deeper.Learning to trust your emotions means honoring them instead of dismissing them as "too sensitive." They are messages pointing you toward what you need.

Believe it or not, journaling is a powerful way to reconnect with your inner voice. Through writing, you avoid overthinking and helps you uncover what you truly want.
These are some of suggestions for you to try:
- "What do I need more of in my life right now?"
- "Where do I feel most at peace?"
- "What situations make me feel drained, and why?"
- "If I stopped worrying about others' opinions, what would I choose?"

Journaling is not about perfect sentences. It's about honesty. Even scribbles or bullet points can reveal your truth.

How to Stop Overthinking and People-Pleasing

Overthinking and pleasing other people often distracts your inner voice. They make you doubt yourself and prioritize others' needs over your own. In overthinking, you replay conversations, worry about every decision, and delay action. Make sure to pause and ask, "What's the simplest next step I can take?" Action quiets overthinking.
In pleasing other people, you say "yes" when you want to say "no," fear of rejection.
Practice small "no's." Start with low-stakes situations, like declining an extra task at work. Each time you honor your needs, your inner voice grows stronger. For example, A friend asks you to help when you're exhausted. Instead of automatically saying yes, you pause, listen to your body, and respond, "I need rest tonight." That moment of honesty is your inner voice guiding you.

Gentle exercises for yourself

Inner Voice Connection

1. Sit quietly for 5 minutes. Notice your breath.
2. Ask yourself: "What do I need right now?"
3. Write down the first answer that comes — without judgment.
4. Reflect: Did the answer surprise you? Did it feel true?

Your inner voice is like a trusted friend who never leaves. The more you listen, the louder it becomes. Reconnecting with it means slowing down, honoring your emotions, and practicing honesty with yourself. Over time, you'll find that decisions feel clearer, relationships feel healthier, and life feels more aligned with who you truly are.

"I trust my inner voice. It guides me with wisdom, clarity, and peace."

AFFIRMATION

CHAPTER 8
Becoming the main character of your Life

Romanticizing Routines, Self-Care, and Small Joys. Being the main character of your life means treating everyday moments as meaningful, not mundane. Romanticizing routines is about slowing down and finding beauty in the ordinary.

Instead of rushing through your morning coffee, you savor it — noticing the warmth of the cup, the aroma, the quiet moment before the day begins. Self-care doesn't have to be extravagant. It can be as simple as taking a walk after work, journaling before bed, or lighting a candle while you read. These small joys remind you that your life is worth celebrating every day.

Designing Your "New Era" of Habits. Every main character has a turning point — a moment where they decide to step into a new chapter. Your "new era" habits are the small, intentional changes that reflect the person you're becoming. You decide that in your new era, you'll stop checking your phone first thing in the morning. Instead, you'll start with gratitude by saying, "Thank God! I'm alive!", It's another beautiful day again!", journaling or stretching.

Habits don't have to be dramatic. Even one shift — like drinking more water, practicing affirmations, or setting boundaries — signals to yourself: "I am stepping into a new season of growth."

Exercises to Identify Personal Goals and Values

To live as the main character, you need clarity about what matters most to you. Identifying your goals and values helps you design a life that feels authentic.
- ***Exercise 1 Values Check-In***: Write down your top 5 values (e.g., peace, creativity, family, freedom, growth). Simple ask: "Am I living in alignment with these values?"
- ***Exercise 2 Future Self Visualization***:Close your eyes and imagine yourself one year from now. What habits, relationships, and routines make you feel proud? Write them down.
- ***Exercise 3: Goal Mapping:*** Choose one small goal that reflects your values. For example, if creativity is a value, commit to painting once a week. If peace is a value, commit to 10 minutes of meditation daily.

If your value is "freedom," your goal might be saving money for solo travel. If your value is "connection," your goal might be scheduling weekly calls with loved ones.

Becoming the main character of your life is not about perfection or performance. It's about choosing to see yourself as worthy of joy, growth, and celebration. When you romanticize routines, design habits that reflect your new era, and align your goals with your values, you stop living passively and start living intentionally.

Remember you are not a side character in someone else's story. You are the author and the lead.

"I am the main character of my life. My routines, habits, and goals reflect my worth."

AFFIRMATION

CHAPTER 9
Real-Life Hacks for Confidence and Peace

Confidence and peace often slip away when stress takes over. Grounding techniques are simple tools that bring you back to the present moment, reminding your body and mind that you are safe. I will share to you some quick grounding techniques, Stress Hacks, and Emotional Resets that you can try.

- **Breathing Reset**: Inhale for 4 counts, hold for 4, exhale for 6. This slows your nervous system. For example, you're about to give a presentation and feel shaking. A few rounds of this breathing exercise calm your body and steady your voice.
- **5-4-3-2-1 Technique**: Name 5 things you see, 4 you feel, 3 you hear, 2 you smell, 1 you taste. For example, during an argument, instead of spiraling or repeating again or recalling the argument, you use this technique to anchor yourself in the present. This helps you remember: "I am worthy of respect, even in disagreement."
- **Mini Reset Rituals**: Step outside for fresh air, splash water on your face, or stretch for 2 minutes. For example, after a stressful work call, you take a short walk to reset before moving on.

These hacks don't remove stress, but it can stop controlling yourself. It helps you gain back that power you had in the moment.

Confidence and peace grow when you protect your energy. This means being intentional about what you allow into your life. You can say Yes to relationships that uplift you, activities that bring joy and calm and opportunities that align with your values. Most importantly, you can say No to overcommitment that drains you, conversations that feel toxic and obligations that don't serve your growth.

Imagine this, a friend invites you to a late-night outing, but you're exhausted. Instead of forcing yourself, you say, "No, I need rest tonight." Protecting your energy allows you to show up stronger tomorrow. Every "no" to what drains you is a "yes" to your peace. Boundaries are energy protectors.

Gentle exercises for yourself

Confidence & Peace Toolkit

1. Write down 3 grounding techniques you'll use when stress rises.
2. Choose 2 affirmations to repeat daily.
3. List 3 things you'll say "yes" to this week and 3 things you'll say "no" to.

Having confidence and peace is not about living a challenge-free life — that's impossible. Stress may knock in you door, but it doesn't have to move in, In life, there are unexpected changes, and moments of doubt. The difference lies in how you respond. When you have tools to ground yourself, affirm your worth, and protect your energy, challenges stop being overwhelming. Instead, they become opportunities to practice resilience, clarity and calm.

Grounding techniques remind you that you are safe and capable in the present moment. They stop your mind from racing into "what ifs" and bring you back to "what is." One example also of this technique are affirmations. These are daily reminders that your value is not defined by circumstances or other people's opinions. They strengthen your inner voice so that when challenges arise, you don't crumble under self-doubt.

Challenges may come, but they do not define me. I face them with confidence, peace, and self-worth."

AFFIRMATION

CHAPTER 10
Maintaining Self-Worth and Emotional Freedom

Regaining self-worth is not a single moment of awakening — it is a consistent practice, a gentle returning to yourself day after day. In this chapter, we explore weekly check-ins, reflection prompts, and self-love rituals that help you stay rooted in your truth, even when life gets loud or overwhelming. Think of this as your safe place — a space where you learn to listen to your emotions without judgment, respond to yourself with compassion, and make decisions from strength rather than fear. I would like to remind you, that self-worth grows when you consistently show up for yourself, honouring your needs, your pace, and your progress. Along the way, you will learn to create regular moments of quiet reflection, to hold yourself through emotional waves, and to celebrate every small victory that proves you are becoming the person you have always deserved to be.

How to Handle Setbacks Gently

Setbacks are not signs of failure — they are invitations to practice compassion toward yourself. Healing is rarely a straight line; it loops, dips, pauses, and accelerates in unexpected ways. When old memories resurface or you find yourself reacting in familiar but unwanted patterns, your first response should be gentleness, not judgment. Acknowledge what you're feeling and remind yourself: "This is a moment of growth, not defeat."

Take a pause and three slow breaths, allow your mind back into the present moment. Reflect on what triggered the emotional slip and ask yourself, "What do I need right now to feel safe and supported?" This shifts your energy from self-blame to self-soothing.

Then, reframe the setback as feedback rather than a step backward. You are learning new emotional skills, and learning takes repetition. Celebrate your ability to notice the moment and redirect yourself with kindness — that awareness alone is a sign of powerful transformation.

Encouraging Closure: Embracing Your Ongoing Journey

Closure is not a single event — it unfolds slowly, through repeated acts of choosing yourself. It's in the boundaries you set, the truths you accept, and the peace you create internally. True closure doesn't require you to forget what happened; it asks you to reinterpret your past through strength rather than pain.

This chapter guides you toward a healthy, empowered understanding of closure. You will learn how to release emotional attachments that keep you tied to old versions of yourself. You'll practice rituals of letting go — writing letters you don't send, releasing guilt that does not belong to you, and embracing gratitude for the lessons that shaped your resilience.

As you move forward, remember that your journey is not only about becoming someone new — it's also about returning to the woman you were always meant to be. Closure gives you permission to move with lighter steps, clearer boundaries, and a stronger sense of identity. You may still have moments of doubt, but they no longer define you. Instead, they remind you of how far you've come.

Weekly Check-Ins: Staying Connected to Yourself

A weekly self-check helps you stay aware of your needs, emotions, and growth. It doesn't need to be complicated 5 to 10 minutes is enough.

Start it by asking yourself:
- What made me feel proud this week?
- What drained my energy and why?
- Did I honor my boundaries?
- What do I need more of? Less of?
- What is one small thing I can do next week for myself?

Weekly Self-Worth Journal Prompt

"This week, I honored myself by…"
"This week, I want to treat myself with kindness by…"

These small reflections keep you aligned with your healing journey.

Self-Love Rituals to Keep You Grounded

Rituals help you reconnect with your identity, your worth, and your emotional peace.
Try these simple weekly rituals:
- A slow morning routine with affirmations
- A short walk without your phone
- A 10-minute "unplug" moment before bed

- Decluttering one small area of your space
- Writing a love note to yourself
- Celebrating small wins with something symbolic (a treat, a break, a candle)

Self-Love Affirmation Ritual: Say this gently:

"I am worthy of peace, love, and respect. I choose myself today."
Repeating this regularly strengthens your emotional foundation.

"I let go of what no longer serves my peace, and I welcome the woman I am becoming."

Your self-worth journey is continuous—soft, evolving, and uniquely yours. You're not rushing. You're not behind. You're growing at the exact pace you were meant to.

You are unbreakable. Not because you never struggled, but because you continue to rise. Maintaining your self-worth is an act of love toward yourself—one choice, one moment, one day at a time.

New year
New lessons
ENDLESS POSSIBILITIES FOR 2026

FINAL ENCOURAGEMENT *Letter*

From the author,

My dear reader,

If you are holding this final page, I want you to pause for a moment and truly acknowledge yourself. You've shown courage which not everyone can claim — the courage to grow, heal, question old patterns, and choose a future where your self-worth is no longer negotiable.

Healing is not a race. It is not linear. And it is not supposed to look perfect. Some days you will feel strong, and other days you may feel tender or overwhelmed. Both are part of becoming the woman you are meant to be.

Please remember this:

> You are worthy even on the days you feel unsure.
> You are strong even when you feel tired.
> You are becoming even when you can't see the progress yet.

Take what you've learned here, hold the tools close, and use them gently. You are building a life where you no longer apologize for your needs, silence your voice, or shrink to make others comfortable.

Walk forward with softness and strength — both belong to you.

With love,

Your Guide

SELF WORTH
Commitment Page

My Self-Worth Commitment

I choose myself.
I choose my peace.
I choose to walk away from what harms my spirit.
I choose boundaries that protect my heart.
I choose to speak kindly to myself.
I choose growth that feels safe and steady.
I choose a life where my worth is not up for debate.

You can freely add your own commitment below:

_____   _____
_____   _____
_____   _____
_____   _____
_____   _____
_____   _____
_____   _____
_____   _____
_____   _____
_____   _____
_____   _____
_____   _____
_____   _____
_____   _____
_____   _____
_____   _____
_____   _____
_____   _____

Signature: _____
Date: _____

30 DAYS SELF WORTH *Challenge*

A Gentle, Fun Reset for Your Mind, Heart & Habits

Day 1: Write 3 things you love about yourself.
Day 2: Clean one small space for mental clarity.
Day 3: Delete a draining contact or mute them.
Day 4: Drink water and rest intentionally.
Day 5: Write one boundary you need.
Day 6: Spend 20 minutes outdoors.
Day 7: Compliment yourself out loud.
Day 8: Write "I deserve peace" 5 times.
Day 9: Unfollow an account that bothers or makes you compare.
Day 10: Do one thing slowly and mindfully.
Day 11: Treat yourself to something small.
Day 12: Replace one negative thought with a kind one.
Day 13: Journal: What am I ready to release?
Day 14: Listen to uplifting music.
Day 15: Write a love note to your future self.
Day 16: Practice saying "No" to something small.
Day 17: Choose a self-care activity.
Day 18: Forgive yourself for one thing.
Day 19: Take a break from your phone for one hour.
Day 20: Celebrate a small win.
Day 21: Visualize who you want to become.
Day 22: Write a promise to yourself.
Day 23: Do something creative.
Day 24: Practice positive posture (stand tall).
Day 25: Do something kind for your body.
Day 26: Journal: What makes me feel safe?
Day 27: Speak one affirmation every hour.
Day 28: Let go of one expectation.
Day 29: Rest without guilt.
Day 30: Reflect on how much you've grown.

REFLECTION
Worksheet

Worksheet 1: What I Learned About Myself

I now understand that..._____

I realized I've been carrying..._____

One thing I no longer believe about myself is..._____

The positive truth I embrace now is..._____

Worksheet 2: My New Boundaries List

I will no longer tolerate..._____

I deserve relationships that..._____

I feel most safe when..._____

My top 3 non-negotiables are..._____

Worksheet 3: Patterns I'm Releasing

A habit I'm letting go of..._____

A mindset that hurt me..._____

A behavior I want to change..._____

My healthier replacement is..._____

SELF WORTH
Trackers

SELF-WORTH TRACKER – WEEKLY CHECK-IN

Week of: _____

A. Daily Self-Worth Rating
How worthy, grounded, or confident did you feel today? (1 = drained, 5 = empowered)

Day	Rating (1–5)	Why I Felt This Way
Monday	___	_____
Tuesday	___	_____
Wednesday	___	_____
Thursday	___	_____
Friday	___	_____
Saturday	___	_____
Sunday	___	_____

B. My Three Self-Worth Wins This Week
(Small or big — they all matter)

1.
2.
3.

C. What Drained My Worth This Week?
(People, habits, thoughts, situations)

_____

D. How Did I Support Myself Emotionally?
(Healthy coping skills, boundaries, rest, saying no, etc.)

_____
_____
_____

E. Self-Worth Affirmations I Practiced
(Circle or write your own)

- I deserve peace.
- I deserve respect.
- I am enough.
- I am learning to love myself.
- My worth is not defined by others.
- I choose me.
- I am safe to grow and evolve.

My own affirmation: _____

F. Self-Love Habits Checklist
(Tick what you completed)

- ☐ Drank enough water
- ☐ Slept properly
- ☐ Took breaks
- ☐ Said "no" when needed
- ☐ Reduced contact with draining people
- ☐ Spent time alone
- ☐ Practiced gratitude
- ☐ Protected my boundaries
- ☐ Did something fun
- ☐ Spoke kindly to myself

G. My Self-Worth Goal for Next Week
A small, achievable goal that supports my emotional growth:

_____
_____
_____
_____
_____
_____
_____
_____

H. A Gentle Promise to Myself
"I promise to..."

_____
_____
_____

PRINTABLE
Affirmation Cards

"My worth is not up for debate."
"I choose peace over pressure."
"I am enough exactly as I am."
"I walk away from anything that dims my light."
"Healing is my new beginning."
"I deserve safe love — especially from myself."
"Being single doesn't mean being incomplete."
"I am becoming stronger every day."

PRINTABLE
Affirmation Cards

ABOUT THE *Author*

Hello beautiful soul — and welcome.

I am Zandra Mae, call me Zandy for short and I write to you not as a counselor, mentor, coach, and educator, but also as a woman and mother who has walked through seasons of doubt, healing, rebuilding, and rediscovery. I've supported women from different walks of life — young professionals, single mothers, survivors of difficult relationships, and women simply trying to find themselves again in a noisy world.

Through my journey as a teacher, mentor, and guide, I've witnessed something powerful: When a woman learns her worth, she becomes unstoppable and unbreakable. But I've also seen how hard it can be to talk about self-worth — even when surrounded by friends or family. Many women carry silent battles, private fears, and emotional scars they've never spoken aloud.

I created this book to give you the safe space you deserve. A space where you are heard, understood, and supported without judgment. You don't need to have everything together. You don't need to be perfect. You just need the willingness to begin. And I'm here to take that journey with you — gently, one chapter at a time.

CONNECT WITH *Me*

Let's Connect!

I share daily reminders, journal prompts, tools, and encouragement. If you like, Join the community:

✉ Email: _zandramaecochrane@gmail.com

"Thank you for letting my words be part of your healing."

You are not broken. You are becoming.

If you've ever questioned your worth, doubted your place, or stayed in spaces that dimmed your light, this book was made for you.

Unbreakable and Becoming is a gentle guide in your hands — guiding you through self-love, boundaries, emotional healing, and rediscovering the woman you were always meant to be.

Inside You'll Find: One-page, beginner-friendly chapters, Practical tips & real-life examples, Fun self-worth challenges and activities, Worksheets, trackers, and self-love rituals and Affirmations you can return to anytime

This is your safe space, your fresh start, and your reminder that your worth has never left you — you're simply reclaiming it.

Take a deep breath.

You're becoming someone beautifully unbreakable.

www.ingramcontent.com/pod-product-compliance
Lightning Source LLC
Chambersburg PA
CBHW061732070526
44583CB00024B/3109